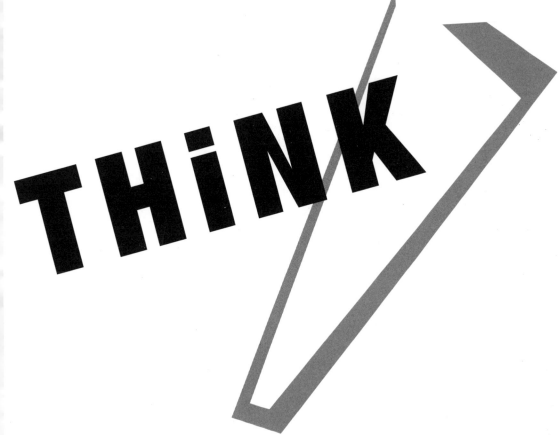

THiNK

BEFORE YOU ACT

Thinking skills and behaviour improvement for 9 to 16 year-olds.
An activity based approach.

Michael Hymans

Lucky Duck is more than a publishing house and training agency. George Robinson and Barbara Maines founded the company in the 1980's when they worked together as a head and psychologist developing innovative strategies to support challenging students.

They have an international reputation for their work on bullying, self-esteem, emotional literacy and many other subjects of interest to the world of education.

George and Barbara have set up a regular news-spot on the website. Twice yearly these items will be printed as a newsletter. If you would like to go on the mailing list to receive this then please contact us:

Lucky Duck Publishing Ltd, 3 Thorndale Mews, Clifton, Bristol, BS8 2HX, UK

Phone: 0044 (0)117 973 2881   e-mail newsletter@luckyduck.co.uk

Fax: 044 (0)117 973 1707   website www.luckyduck.co.uk

ISBN 1 904 315 05 4

Published by Lucky Duck Publishing Ltd
3 Thorndale Mews, Clifton, Bristol, BS8 2HX, UK

www.luckyduck.co.uk

Commissioning Editor: George Robinson
Editor: Mel Maines
Designer: Helen Weller
Illustrator: Philippa Drakeford

Printed by Antony Rowe Limited

Acknowledgement

A special acknowledgement must be given to Edward de Bono whose original work on CoRT Thinking inspired my teaching of children presenting with hostile and inconsequential behaviour during the late 1970's and early 1980's. Think Before You Act draws heavily on the ideas within the CoRT Thinking material and later work by de Bono for developing tools for thinking. I believe that my programme of lessons provides children with opportunities to practise their thinking in a familiar and up-to-date context without detracting from the original de Bono concept of broadening perceptions and using creativity in the treatment of ideas. The modern and 'attractive' presentation of teaching and learning materials should motivate children with and without behaviour problems to actively participate in lessons and should enable the teacher to mediate in the children's thinking process as suggested by de Bono and other authors in the field of teaching thinking skills.

The CD-ROM

The CD-ROM contains PDF files of the worksheets for each lesson and full-colour versions of the posters from the Appendix. You will need Acrobat Reader version 3 or higher to view and print these resources. You will find three files on the CD-ROM labelled: Worksheets.pdf and Lesson Posters.pdf and Thinking Caps.pdf. Each lesson contents will direct you to the page to print from the file Lesson Posters.pdf for each lessons corresponding poster. The number of each worksheet corresponds to the page number in the file Worksheets.pdf.

The documents are set up to print to A4 but you can enlarge them to A3 by increasing the output percentage at the point of printing using the page set-up settings for your printer.

Alternatively, you may wish to take the CD-ROM to a local company that offers print services.

Contents

Introduction

In recent years there has been an increasing amount of time given to the idea that schools should be less concerned with imparting information and more concerned with encouraging the kind of teaching which pays attention to the way children learn. There has also been an increasing realisation that children's thinking abilities, such as asking relevant questions, seeing connections between different strands of thought and generalising from particular instances in order to draw out the consequences of what is said and done, are underestimated.

There is also a general view that the way children feel is related to the manner in which they perform in the classroom. *"We have gone too far in emphasising the value and importance of the purely rational - what IQ measures - intelligence can come to nothing when emotions hold sway."* (Daniel Goleman, 1996). High self-esteem provides a child with the confidence to attempt difficult things without an incapacitating fear of failure. In contrast, children with low self-esteem find it difficult to try new strategies. They protect what they have and continue to behave in a manner consistent with their poor view of themselves.

According to Lane (1990), children displaying various forms of attention-seeking behaviour and described as 'impossible' to teach by their teachers have an unawareness of, and/or disregard for, the consequences of their actions. These children fail to inhibit the first aggressive responses, to frustration or dominance over age-peers, that come to their mind. Such children act impulsively without an advanced mental rehearsal of the consequences, so that the trials and errors that take place do so in actual dealings with others and their behaviour is often harmful or annoying. They are forgetful of the bad results of previous actions in the past and in learning tasks they similarly act by trial-and-error or guessing: since this is often ineffective they become discouraged and possibly antagonistic. These children will often try and avoid learning through a gamut of displacement activities such as disturbing others, clowning around and making excuses for leaving their seat or the classroom. Many of these pupils have difficulty generalising newly acquired skills such as those gained from 'counselling' in the classroom and school environment.

Similarly, most children are unlikely to test and demonstrate their ability to think in particular ways and in particular circumstances if they do not believe that such thinking is either possible or permissible for them. The National Curriculum with its teacher assessments and SATs often demonstrates what children and young people do not know. Thinking skills programmes are concerned with what happens when children and young people do not know. Hymans (1994) suggested that teaching thinking skills can also significantly reduce attention-seeking behaviour as well as having applications across all National Curriculum subjects. This study described a thinking skills project that was carried out in a special school catering for the needs of children aged 5-11 years experiencing emotional, social and behavioural difficulties and in a mainstream primary school. Two educational psychologists taught eight 9 and 10 year olds the original version of De Bono's introduction to the CoRT Thinking Programme in the special school and this author taught the same programme to a class of 10 and 11 year olds in the mainstream school. The Bristol Social Adjustment Guides, Child in School, was used pre- and post-teaching intervention and a contingency management reinforcement schedule was completed by a non-participant observer. The results showed that teaching a Thinking Skills programme to the children in the special school significantly reduced their inconsequential and over-reactive behaviour. The same results were found with an identified sample of children in the mainstream school. This led to the author proposing that teaching children to 'think before they act' could have applications in both special and mainstream schools and could have applications to new and unfamiliar situations across the whole curriculum including the National Curriculum.

Nevertheless, the idea that thinking skills are developed as a by-product of, for example, Geography and History, is no longer tenable according to De Bono (1986). He concludes that such descriptive thinking is not enough because the thinking required for action must include, for example, consideration of 'priorities', 'objectives' and 'other people's views'. When children make use of these they dictate what is debated and how the debate is conducted and when used in a social context, with an adult acting as a mediator, each child can have equal importance and can contribute and gain from a climate of enquiry in which favourable attitudes and dispositions can be fostered in a natural way.

The research on the relationship between reflectivity and inferential skills by Kagan, Pearson and Welch (1966) and Kagan's (1965) studies of 'reflectivity/impulsivity' suggest that cognitive style is something different from intelligence. Both De Bono (1993) and Feurenstein (1979) have dispelled the myth that a person with a high IQ is likely to be an effective thinker. For De Bono, intelligence is the innate horsepower of a car and thinking skills are equivalent to the essential driving skills.

Rationale

The rationale for adopting an approach based on De Bono's (1986) CoRT Thinking Skills materials is the high premium that is placed on children's own ideas. This not only enables skills to be taught but also encourages the cognitive and affective disposition to use the skills as in showing respect for other people, readiness to consider alternative explanations, care for the process of enquiry, readiness to listen to others and habits of self-appraisal and sensible agreement.

The teacher acts as the mediator in order to help children understand their own way of thinking and to negotiate the gap between experience and objectives. The purpose of this approach is to enable children to apply newly acquired thinking (skills) to different and unfamiliar situations that have to be faced. The ultimate aim is very similar to that of a sports coach, that is, to make the basic operations of thinking second nature so that they are carried out without fuss or effort.

The simplest form of thinking is to react to a situation. The next stage is to enlarge the way we look at that situation or to broaden perception. De Bono's approach highlights two ways of broadening perception, to know more about the situation and add more detail, and to try and find different ways of looking at the same situation instead of assuming there is only one right way.

The lessons that follow help children to enlarge their view of the situation by encouraging them to think about more aspects as well as encouraging them to find different ways of looking at that same situation. These lessons have been used successfully in a number of both mainstream and special primary and secondary schools.

The Benefits

The delivery of this thinking skills programme enables teachers to assess and gain a better understanding of the range and development of creative and lateral thinking within the class. It enables children to see that there is more than one answer and that they can offer a range of responses to questions - they can think 'outside the box.' As children begin to value each others' ideas they gain confidence and are more willing to participate. Teachers notice the inclusion of a wider range of ideas within children's creative writing.

The impetus for producing this programme was based on experiences gained from teaching so called 'disruptive' (7-15) year olds in two off-site units, which are now more commonly named Pupil Referral Units, during the late 1970s and early 1980s. The rationale being that traditional interventions such as counselling fail to help students generalise newly acquired skills in a range of settings inside and outside the classroom. School settings continue to aim to help students gain knowledge through accessing a broad and balanced curriculum. However, examinations and teacher assessments frequently demonstrate what pupils do not know.

This programme is concerned with what happens when children and young people 'do not know', a problem constantly facing the 'low-achieving' student, the 'average' student and the 'gifted' student alike. It is common to all of us that, when we do not know, we need to think and we need to learn. A focus on thinking skills may reduce the chances of children and young people saying:

"It's not that I haven't learnt much, it's just I don't understand what I'm doing."

Using thinking skills programmes with the students in the off-site units promoted a learning orientation that led to a positive pattern of motivation, in that there was:

▬ A belief amongst the students that effort leads to success.

▬ A belief in the students' own ability to improve and learn.

▬ A satisfaction gained from personal success at difficult tasks.

The original materials used with these students were aimed at reducing their attention-seeking and impulsive behaviours, and teaching them to behave in more reflective and thoughtful ways - especially as there is a strong case, empirical and theoretical (Jones, 1988; Lake 1988), for a programme of this type to be effective in aiding children and young people's social adjustment.

This programme is relevant to everyday real life events and rests easily within the 'citizenship' curriculum. The acquisition of thinking tools can be generalised to both Core and Foundation subjects within the National Curriculum. The programme can be used with children and young people at the upper end of primary schools and right through secondary schools.

Teaching Methodology and How to Use the Programme

Groupings

The pupils/students work in groups that can be put together by dividing the class into groups that the teacher thinks would work best. Arbitrary arrangements can be made according to seating organisation or with highly motivated pupils/students natural groups can be formed in which a group of friends work together. An alternative arrangement is for the teacher to have pupils/students pick up slips of paper to assign them to a particular group. In general, the more articulate the class the smaller the group size and small groups that do not produce very much can be re-grouped into larger groups. The ideal group size is between four and six. It is a good idea to ask the groups to select a spokesperson before the start of each activity. The teacher may nominate a different person each time in order to give everyone a chance to express the ideas of the group. However, there is little point in forcing a reluctant pupil/student to do this. The groups can be changed from time to time, say after every three lessons, and minor switches can be made if there are personality clashes or the teacher notices that a group is particularly weak.

The groups discuss the situation (practice item) they have been asked to think about and develop their own ideas and conclusions. One group is designated to give its output via the spokesperson whilst other groups listen and add their own ideas, comments or disagreements when invited to by the teacher. The output is usually verbal but there is flexibility within the programme for written comments either during the lesson or via homework as a means of follow-up reinforcement activities.

The fundamental principle of all lessons is that no single practice item should occupy too much time, however fascinating the discussion, in order to force pupils/students to shift their attention from content to the thinking process. The lessons should run at a fast pace and the teacher must keep control of the output. Teachers can comment on ideas or cut off a discussion and move on to the next item. They can choose to ask any group or individual for a comment or choose not to in order to maintain the pace and flow.

Content

It is not easy to predict what content will interest a particular class and so in each lesson teachers may choose from a selection of practice items to find the ones best suited to their classes. Sometimes teachers make the mistake of assuming that, since there is no one right answer, they cannot judge the ideas offered and must accept them all. There is no one right answer but there are many possible right answers. There are also many wrong answers or trivial answers and teachers are perfectly justified in treating them as such.

However, teachers must not dismiss ideas just because they are different from their own. It is also the case that teachers are not really judging ideas but judging whether pupils/students are practising thinking. The thinking lessons are no different from lessons in other subjects which do not have absolute answers. So, in the same way, teachers should make the lessons interesting, maintain control and a brisk pace and give pupils/students a definite sense of achievement. The main difference with thinking skills lessons is the need for the teacher to keep the focus on the process rather than the content and to remember that the purpose of the lessons is to develop thinking as a skill or tool that can be applied to any situation. It is not about having general discussions on interesting topics.

Time

The lessons are designed to be used once a week for a term (12 weeks) with a lesson time of approximately 55 minutes. The extent of the teacher's mediating or facilitating role will vary according to the age and ability of the pupils/students, the type of class and their level of motivation. Teachers can comment and elaborate on ideas put forward. They can link one idea with another or contrast them and they can work on them and develop the interest in them. The guidelines presented in this programme give teachers the freedom to discuss and expand ideas with their classes.

Resources

The only resources used are those already present in the minds of the pupils/students. Thinking is the skilled use of already available information so the pupils/students are not required to absorb written or any other form of visual material before they can start thinking. Worksheets are provided to aid small group discussion and whole-class feedback.

Structure

Each lesson has the same basic structure, other than Lessons 5 and 6, although the content within this structure varies widely. Lessons 5 and 6 follow a different structure as the 'thinking tool' is broken down into two parts. In all other lessons the expectation is that the use of the thinking tool will be completed within the allotted time for the lesson with the freedom to use follow-up activities in an appropriate way, for example, as homework. Each of the lessons comprises the following basic sections:

Introduction: This explains the particular aspect of thinking covered in that lesson and provides an example.

Group activity: This provides problems and situations to practise thinking.

Process: This describes and/or opens class discussion on the aspect of thinking and/or type of thinking tool that is the subject of that lesson.

Principles: This gives up to five basic principles concerning the subject of the lesson for groups to examine and comment upon.

Project: This provides further problems and thinking situations that can be tackled at that time or later.

References

De Bono, E. (1999) *Six Thinking Hats*, Penguin Books.

De Bono, E. (1993) *Teach Your Child How To Think*, Penguin Books.

De Bono, E. (1986) *CoRT Thinking* (Teacher's Notes), Book 1: Breadth, MICA Management Resources (UK).

Feurenstein, R.(1979) *The Dynamic Assessment of Retarded Performers: The Learning Potential Device, Theory, Instruments and Techniques*. Baltimore, University Park Press.

Goleman, D. (1996) *Emotional Intelligence: Why it can matter more than IQ*, London, Bloomsbury Publishing.

Hymans, M.H. (1994) Impulsive Behaviour: A case for helping children think about change, *Educational Psychology in Practice*, Vol 10. No 3., Longman.

Jones, S. (1988) Self-Esteem, Collaborative Learning and Lipman's Philosophy for Children Programme, *Links* (Spring) 33-36.

Kagan, J. (1965) Reflection Impulsivity and Reading Ability in Primary Grade Children, *Child Development* 36, 609-628.

Kagan, J., Pearson, L. and Welch, L. (1966) Conceptual Impulsivity and Inductive Reasoning, *Child Development* 37(3), 583-594.

Lake, M. (1988) Group Participation Compared with Individual Problem-Solving, *Thinking Skills Newsletter*, 5, 12-16.

Lane, D.A. (1990) *The Impossible Child*, Nottingham, Trentham Books.

Michalko, M. (2001) *Cracking Creativity: The Secrets of Creative Genius*, California, Ten Speed Press.

Stephenson, D. (2001) *Creative Thinking: A course in creative thinking for all ages*, Essex, Clare Publications.

Stott, D.H. (1974) *Manual of the Bristol Social Adjustment Guides: The Social Adjustment of Children* (5th Edition) [OP]; *Child in School*, London, Hodder and Stoughton.

Wallace, B, Ed. (2001) *Teaching Thinking Skills Across the Primary Curriculum: A practical approach for all abilities*, London, David Fulton Publishers.

Lesson 1:

Introduction to the Programme

What is thinking?

Introduction
(10 minutes)

Tell the story of the Hungry Man.
Introduce the Six Thinking Caps
(10 minutes).

Group activity
(20 minutes)

Practising using the Thinking Caps with the prompt sheet: *Questions asked of the Six Thinking Caps*.

Process
(10 minutes)
the

Re-iterating the definitions of the Thinking Caps and *Questions asked of*

Six Thinking Caps.

Principles
(2 minutes)

What the thinking in today's lesson has been used for.

Project

Some more examples of practising using the Thinking Caps.

Resources

Prompt sheet: *Questions asked of the Six Thinking Caps*.

Worksheets 1–5.

Thinking Caps.pdf posters.

Introduction

Teacher:

The simplest form of thinking is to react to a situation.

> A hungry man stumbles across a deserted castle. It is late at night and he is cold and tired. He goes inside the castle and sees a plate on the table with a whole chicken on it. What should he do?

Take some answers and then continue the story:

> Although the castle is deserted, the man remembers being told that someone might still be living there. What should he do now?

Take some answers and then continue the story:

> The hungry man looks all around the castle and discovers that there is actually no-one living in the castle right now. He believes that the chicken might be infected. What should he do now?

Take some answers and then continue the story:

> The hungry man gave a piece of chicken to a Blackbird who then ate it and did not seem to be affected in any way. The hungry man knows that he still has a long way to go on his journey and is not sure what he should do next. Can you think of any suggestions for him?

Take some answers and then make the following comments to the group:

> In each case of the story the immediate situation is the same (the chicken on the plate), but the 'enlarged' view of the same situation is very different. The simplest thing for the hungry man to do is to react to the situation (the chicken on the plate): he can identify the situation and react to it. However, if he enlarges the way he looks at the situation (the chicken on the plate) he broadens his understanding. It does not tell him how to react, but it may change what he is reacting to.

> The thinking lessons that follow over the next 11 weeks are designed to enlarge the way we look at a thinking situation. They do not direct what should be done because when we can see the enlarged situation we can act in whatever way seems best.

Thinking Tools

Teacher:

> The Six Thinking Caps are tools that we can use to help enlarge the view of a situation. They can also help us decide how best to act. They are ways of thinking that are like caps because they can be 'put on' and 'taken off'. They are directions in which our thinking can go. They are not descriptions of people. They allow parallel thinking and prevent arguing before choices are made.

As you go through the description of each cap ask the pupils/students to relate the 'colour' to their experiences by asking for examples:

> What does the colour white remind you of?

1. The White Cap - as in a 'blank sheet of paper' - neutral/objective, relating to facts and figures. The information we have/that is missing and how we get the information we need (with the Hungry Man this is the information he has about the castle and who lives there).

2. The Red Cap - as in 'red with anger' - emotions, feelings and hunches, intuition at this moment (the Hungry Man's first response might be to eat the chicken because he is hungry and there is no-one around).

3. The Black Cap - as in 'sombre' - being cautious and careful.
   Does our thinking fit with the facts, our plans and what we believe in?
   Will it work? What are the weaknesses, dangers and problems? (On thinking about the situation the Hungry Man becomes more cautious, believing that the chicken might be infected.)

4. The Yellow Cap - as in 'sunshine' - being optimistic and positive.
   What are the advantages and benefits of our thinking? Who will benefit? Why it will work? Can it be done and is it worth doing? (Giving a piece of chicken to the Blackbird enabled the Hungry Man to see the advantages and benefits of his thinking.)

5. The Green Cap - as in 'green traffic light' - the 'active cap' for making things happen and making suggestions or exploring new/alternative ideas, solutions or inventions. (The pupils/students were asked to think of alternatives/suggestions for the Hungry Man throughout the activity.)

6. The Blue Cap - as in 'blue sky above us' or 'blue as a cool colour' - taking control and organising. Where are we now? What are we trying to do right now? What do other people think? What do I think about what other people think? How effective is their thinking? How far have we got? What is the next step? (The suggested comments at the end of the story about the Hungry Man reflect Blue Cap Thinking.)

Group Activity

Practising using the Thinking Caps in short sequences

Introduce the pupils/students to the idea of using the Thinking Caps in sequence and in different ways according to the nature of the situation or problem to be solved.

- For a quick assessment of an idea - use Yellow, Black and then Red Cap Thinking.
- To generate ideas - use White and then Green Cap Thinking.
- To improve an existing idea - use Black and then Green Cap Thinking.
- To summarise and spell out the alternatives – use Blue and then Green Hat Thinking.
- To see if thinking has had any benefits - use Blue and then Yellow Cap Thinking.

Practice

This part of the lesson should take no longer than 20 minutes: 5 minutes for group discussion and 15 minutes for feedback.

Divide the class into 5 groups and give each of the groups one of the practice sequences above (from one of the Worksheets 1-5) together with the prompt sheet - Questions asked of the Six Thinking Caps. Each group has 5 minutes to answer the question posed by the situation/problem.

One member from each group feeds back to the rest of the class describing which comments relate to which Cap (see prompt sheet). The rest of the class can add suggestions at the end of the feedback.

Process

Using the 6 Thinking Caps

The 6 Thinking Caps are tools for enlarging the view of a situation and helping us decide how best to act.

The 6 Thinking Caps direct our thinking, they are not descriptions of people.

The 6 Thinking Caps can be used more than once, used in sequence and or in different ways depending on the situation or problem to be solved.

The 6 Thinking Caps allow parallel thinking and prevent us from arguing before choices are made.

A quick resumé of the Thinking Cap definitions:

1. White Cap - neutral/objective
2. Red Cap - emotions, feelings and hunches
3. Black Cap - cautious and careful
4. Yellow Cap - optimistic and positive
5. Green Cap - action, making things happen
6. Blue Cap - taking control and organising.

Principles

We have been using our thinking today in order to:

- see that there is more than one answer to a question
- broaden our perception of situations beyond what is in front of us
- apply new ideas and thinking to a range of different situations
- be ready to listen and respond to other people's ideas and views

Project

- Pupils/students can be given any one or more of the Worksheets that they did not discuss in their groups.

What is Thinking?

Prompt sheet: Questions asked of the Six Thinking Caps

1. White Cap

- What information do we have?
- What information is missing?
- How can we get the information we need?

2. Red Cap

- What do I feel about this?
- What are my emotions about this?
- What are my first hunches/thoughts?

3. Black Cap

- Is it true or false?
- Does it fit with the facts, plans or what I believe in?
- Will it work?
- What are the weaknesses, dangers or problems?

4. Yellow Cap

- What are the advantages or benefits?
- Who will benefit?
- Why should it work?
- Why is this worth doing?
- How can it be done?

5. Green Cap

- What are the new ideas?
- What are the alternatives?
- What are the solutions?
- What ideas can be invented or created?

6. Blue Cap

- Where are we now?
- What is the focus?
- What are we trying to do right now?
- What do other people think?
- What do I think about what other people think?
- How effective is other people's thinking?
- How far have we got?
- What is the next step?

What is Thinking? – Lesson 1, Worksheet 1

A quick assessment of an idea (Yellow/Black/Red):

A coin box should be put on top of the television and anyone who wants to watch a programme must pay per hour. Make a quick assessment of this idea.

What is Thinking? – Lesson 1, Worksheet 2

To generate ideas (White/Green):

If you were organising a competition for finding a champion burger eater, what rules would you make for the competition?

_____

_____

_____

_____

_____

_____

_____

_____

_____

_____

_____

_____

_____

_____

_____

_____

_____

_____

What is Thinking? – Lesson 1, Worksheet 3

To improve an existing idea (Black/Green):

How can you improve on the suggestion that all pupils should spend three months every year earning money?

_____

_____

_____

_____

_____

_____

_____

_____

_____

_____

_____

_____

_____

_____

_____

_____

_____

_____

_____

_____

_____

_____

What is Thinking? – Lesson 1, Worksheet 4

To summarise and spell out the alternatives (Blue/Green):

Some areas around the school are very dirty because people drop litter and cans everywhere. How would you suggest tackling this problem?

What is Thinking? – Lesson 1, Worksheet 5

To see if thinking has had any benefits (Blue/Yellow):

Can you think of an alternative shape for a TV screen and use Yellow Cap Thinking to show the benefits of your new shape?

_____

_____

_____

_____

_____

_____

_____

_____

_____

_____

_____

_____

_____

_____

_____

_____

_____

_____

_____

_____

_____

_____

Lesson 2
Plus Minus Interest (PMI)
The Treatment of Ideas

Introduction
(10 minutes)

Explain what is meant by PMI.

Group activity
(30 minutes)

Practising using PMI.

Process
(5 minutes)

Describe the process involved in using PMI.

Principles
(5 minutes)

Describe the principles behind using PMI as a thinking tool.

Project
(optional)

Use any one or more of the practice items and/or additional items for homework.

Resources

Worksheets 6-9.

Lesson Poster.pfd, page 1.

Introduction

What do we mean by PMI?

P = Plus: The good things about an idea - why we like it.

M = Minus: The bad things about an idea - why we don't like it.

I = Interest: Ideas that are neither good nor bad but we can see where they might lead or what might happen.

Teacher:

> Instead of just saying that you like, or don't like, an idea you can use a PMI. When you use a PMI you give the good points first, then the bad points and then the points that are neither good nor bad but are interesting.
>
> You can use a PMI as a way of treating ideas, suggestions and proposals.
>
> You can ask someone else to do a PMI on your idea or you could do one yourself.

Example

Idea: All seats should be taken out of buses.

Plus (P):   More people can get into each bus.
It would be easier to get on and off the bus.
Buses would be cheaper to make and repair.
Buses would be easier to clean.

Minus (M):   Passengers might fall over if the bus stopped suddenly.
Old people and disabled people might not be able to use buses.
It would be difficult to carry shopping bags or babies.

Interest (I): It might lead to three types of buses - one with seats, one without seats and one with seats on the lower or upper deck.
Buses without seats would do more work.
Comfort may not be so important on buses - especially for short journeys.

Group Activity

Practising PMI

> **People should wear badges showing whether they are in a good mood or a bad mood that day.**

Divide the class into groups of 4-6 pupils. Ask each group to nominate a pupil to write answers on Worksheet 6. Tell each group to do a full PMI for 5 minutes (this time can be extended for longer lessons). Tell each group that they can offer one suggestion at a time for either P, M or I points and indicate to them when they have guessed one of the target points. When no more suggestions are forthcoming inform the class of any remaining. (Allow 5 minutes for group feedback - this time can be extended for longer lessons).

Target points

Suggestions (NB - not necessarily the 'right' or 'best' answers).

P: You could keep clear of people in a bad mood.

People might make more of an effort not to be in a bad mood.

M: People would not be honest about wearing the right badge.

Those people wearing 'bad mood' badges would be avoided when they might really need cheering up.

I: You can tell some people's moods from their faces anyway.

Do people prefer to hide their moods or show them?

> **Pupils should vote on their teachers at the end of the school year by giving their teachers a score out of ten.**

Either keep the same groups or change them around. Ask each group to list either P, M or I points on Worksheet 7. Tell them that they have 5 minutes again for this activity. Ask one group to give its Plus points and allow other groups or individuals to add further points. Ask another group to give its Minus points and finally ask a further group to give its Interesting points (allow 5 minutes for group feedback - this time can be extended for longer lessons).

> **What do you think of the idea that for one full week each year children should run their home completely? This would include shopping, cooking and cleaning.**

Either keep the same groups or change them around. Ask each group to do a full PMI for 5 minutes using Worksheet 8 and then take feedback as in number 2 above.

Process

PMI

PMI is a 'scanning' thinking tool that is used in sequence: we look in the 'P' direction first, ignoring other points, and then we do the same for 'M' and 'I'.

Black and Yellow Cap Thinking cannot be used, as minus points are included in our thinking. PMI does not have to be logical and can include feelings, so Red and Green Caps can be used instead. We have used a lot of White and Green Cap Thinking in generating ideas. Red Cap Thinking is important when the issue or idea being discussed has an 'emotional' component. Unless emotions are brought out into the open, they can block the thinking process. You could practise this with the class by asking them what they feel about the idea of young people caring for the elderly.

Principles

- Without a PMI, a valuable idea may be rejected because it seems bad at first.

- Without a PMI, we are very unlikely to see the disadvantages of an idea we like very much.

- Without a PMI, most judgements are based on our emotions at the time (Red Cap Thinking) and not on the value of that idea as well (Blue Cap Thinking).

- With a PMI, we decide whether or not we like the idea, after we have explored it and not before.

Project

Other ideas that can be substituted for any one or more of the above practice items or used as follow-up activities/homework.

- Do a PMI on the idea that regular play/break times are abandoned and teachers decide when children should have a break for play

- What do you think of the idea that every young person should adopt an old person to care for?

- A parent thinks that her children are spending too much time playing computer games so she puts a coin box on the computer and anyone who wants to play computer games must pay per hour. What do you think of this idea?

Practising PMI – Lesson 2, Worksheet 6

The Treatment of Ideas

As a group, do a PMI on the following statement:

People should wear badges showing whether they are in a good mood or a bad mood that day.

P

_____

_____

_____

_____

_____

_____

M

_____

_____

_____

_____

_____

_____

I

_____

_____

_____

_____

_____

After 5 minutes we will compare answers.

Practising PMI – Lesson 2, Worksheet 7

The Treatment of Ideas

As a group, do either a P, M or I on the following statement:

Pupils should vote on their teachers at the end of the school year by giving their teachers a score out of ten.

P

_____

_____

_____

_____

M

_____

_____

_____

_____

I

_____

_____

_____

_____

After 5 minutes we will compare answers.

Practising PMI – Lesson 2, Worksheet 8

The Treatment of Ideas

What do you think of the idea that, for one full week each year, children should run their home completely? This would include shopping, cooking and cleaning.

As a group do a PMI on this question:

P

M

I

After 5 minutes we will compare answers.

Lesson 3
Consider All Factors: (CAF)
The Factors Involved

Introduction (10 minutes)	Explain what is meant by CAF and why it is important.
Group activity (40 minutes)	Practising using CAF.
Process (5 minutes)	Describe the process involved in using CAF.
Principles (5 minutes)	Describe the principles behind using CAF as a thinking tool.
Project (optional)	Use any one or more of the practice items and/or additional items for homework.
Resources	Worksheets 9-11. Lesson Posters.pdf, page 2.

Introduction

What do we mean by CAF?

Teacher:

CAF stands for Consider All Factors.

When we have to choose, make a decision or just think about something, there are always many factors that we have to consider:

- factors affecting ourselves
- factors affecting others
- factors affecting our community or society in general.

Why is CAF important?

Teacher:

If we leave out some of these factors our choice may seem right at the time but might later turn out to be wrong. When we are looking at other people's thinking we can try and see what factors they have left out.

Example

Looking around a second-hand car showroom a man suddenly spotted his favourite make of sports car:

- The paintwork was in good condition.
- The tyres were not worn.
- It had a low mileage for its age.
- The engine and other mechanical parts all seemed OK.
- The price was just about affordable.

He was so delighted that he went back later to buy the car and drives home smiling and singing to the music on the car stereo.

When he gets home he finds that the car is too wide for his garage. He had forgotten to do a CAF!

Group Activity

Practising CAF

> **You are asked to design a poster to encourage young people to drink more Coca Cola. What factors do you have to keep in mind?**

Divide the class into groups of 4-6 pupils. Ask each group to nominate a pupil to record answers (on Worksheet 9) and feedback to the whole class. Tell each group to consider all the factors involved in advertising and tell them that they have 10 minutes to do a full CAF. After 10 minutes ask one group to give its answers and allow other groups and individuals to add further points. Allow 10 minutes for feedback.

List all the different points and ask each group to pick out the 4 points they consider to be the most important.

> **An inventor has invented a breakfast pill that contains all the food and vitamins needed so that people taking it will not feel hungry for five hours. What are the factors involved in allowing this pill to be used?**

This is a quick activity. A starting signal is given and in the next two minutes each group must pick out as many factors as possible using Worksheet 10. The group that volunteers the highest number of answers feeds back to the rest of the class to which others can add answers. This is a race to pick out the most factors in the shortest time. Allow 3 minutes for feedback.

Suggestions

■ Can you be sure the pill contains all the ingredients you need?

■ What would happen to all the farmers, food manufacturers and shops?

■ There would be no dishes to wash!

■ Breakfast would not be so enjoyable!

■ Would your stomach shrink?

■ Pills could be used instead of all food!

■ Would the pill be safe? What about side-effects?

> **If you were interviewing someone to be a teacher, what factors would you consider?**

Tell the pupils that there are 5 minutes allowed for this item. Each group provides one factor from Worksheet 11 until all are exhausted. Allow 10 minutes for feedback.

Process

CAF

■ CAF is an 'attention-directing' thinking tool that is designed to increase the breadth of perception (as with Lesson 1 - the Hungry Man and the plate of chicken).

■ There is a difference between important factors and less important factors but the main effort is to find the factors first.

■ Although the attention-directing tool is a very simple tool, it is very powerful when done well!

Principles

Doing a CAF is useful before choosing, deciding or planning.

- It is better to consider all the factors first and then pick out the ones that matter the most.

- You may have to ask someone else to tell you whether you have left out some important factors.

- If you have left out an important factor your answer may seem right but might later turn out to be wrong.

Project

Other ideas that can be substituted for any one or more of the above items or used as follow-up activities/homework.

- What factors do you need to consider in deciding what to do when on holiday from school?

- What factors do you need to consider if you were going to design a chair for young people?

- What things do you have to keep in mind when going for an interview for a job?

Practising CAF – Lesson 3, Worksheet 9

The Factors Involved

You are asked to design a poster to encourage young people to drink more Coca Cola. What factors do you have to keep in mind?

Factors affecting you:

_____

_____

_____

_____

Factors affecting others:

_____

_____

_____

_____

Factors affecting the community and/or society:

_____

_____

_____

_____

The 4 most important factors:

1 _____

2 _____

3 _____

4 _____

After 10 minutes we will compare answers.

Practising CAF – Lesson 3, Worksheet 10

The Factors Involved

An inventor has invented a breakfast pill that contains all the food and vitamins needed so that people taking it will not feel hungry for five hours.

What are the factors involved in allowing this pill to be used?

Factors affecting you:

_____

_____

_____

_____

_____

Factors affecting others:

_____

_____

_____

_____

_____

Factors affecting the community and/or society:

_____

_____

_____

_____

_____

After 2 minutes we will compare answers.

Practising CAF – Lesson 3, Worksheet 11

The Factors Involved

If you were interviewing someone to be a teacher what factors would you consider?

Factors affecting pupils:

_____

_____

_____

_____

_____

Factors affecting other teachers:

_____

_____

_____

_____

_____

Factors affecting parents of children at the school:

_____

_____

_____

_____

_____

After 5 minutes we will compare answers.

Lesson 4
Rules

Introduction (5 minutes)	Explain why it is important to have rules.
Group activity (45 minutes)	Practising using rules.
Process (5 minutes)	Discuss the process involved in using rules.
Principles (5 minutes)	Describe the principles for having rules.
Project (optional)	Use any one or more of the practice items and/or additional items for homework.
Resources	Worksheets 12 & 13. Rough paper (A4). Lesson Posters.pdf, page 3.

Introduction

Why do we have rules?

Teacher:

> Some rules are made to prevent confusion - for example, the rule that cars must drive on one side of the road (reference can be made to the side of the road cars in the UK and other countries must drive on and whether there's any confusion in making the switch).

> Some rules are made to be enjoyed - for example, the rules of football and netball are an important part in making the games enjoyable for both players and spectators.

> Some rules are made by organisations for their own members - for example, the rule that children must wear a uniform at school.

> Some rules are made to prevent a few people from taking advantage of everyone else - for example, the rule that you must not steal.

> In general, the purpose of a rule is to make life easier and better for the majority of people.

Group Activity

Practising Using Rules

If you were running a school which rules would you insist on?

Divide into groups of 4-6 pupils. Ask each group to nominate a pupil to feedback to the whole class. The groups spend 5 minutes trying to produce as many rules as possible and these can be recorded on rough paper. They should be encouraged to use White and Green Cap Thinking - see prompt sheet in Lesson 1, (Questions asked of the Six Thinking Caps) by asking, for example:

- What school rules do we already have?
- What alternative or new rules should we have?

At the end of 5 minutes ask each group in turn for one rule until no further ones are forthcoming. Allow 5 minutes for this feedback.

All responses can be listed. Ask each group to pick one rule from the list and to do a CAF for that rule - recording their responses on Worksheet 12. Allow 5 minutes for this part of the activity.

Encourage pupils to use Yellow, Black and Red Cap Thinking - see prompt sheet from Lesson 1, by asking, for example:

- What are the advantages or benefits of the rule?
- What are the weaknesses, dangers or problems with the rule?
- What do I feel about the rule?

Ask the group with the longest list to give its output, to which others can add to and responses can be listed. Allow 10 minutes for this feedback.

Practising Using Rules

> **Can you think of four main rules parents should follow when managing their children?**

Ask the groups to spend 5 minutes trying to produce (on rough paper) four rules. Ask each group in turn to give one rule until no further rules are forthcoming.

Suggestions

- Parents should listen more.
- Parents should try to see things from a child's point of view.
- Parents should not argue in front of their children.
- Parents should let their children make some decisions for themselves.
- Parents should tell their children what they like about their behaviour from time to time.

Allow the pupils to pick out a single rule to explore by doing a full PMI - see Worksheet 13 (allow 5 minutes for this activity). After 5 minutes select one or two groups to give their outputs and prompt others to add further points.

Allow 5 minutes for feedback.

Process

Based on the responses to the 'practice' items, discuss answers to the following questions - link to 'principles' that follow:

- Which rules are good and which are bad?
- Who should make the rules?
- What are rules for?
- When are rules useful?

Principles

- A rule should be widely known, understood and possible to follow.
- A rule is not a 'bad' rule just because some people do not like it.
- A rule should work for the benefit of those who have to follow it.
- Those who have to follow a rule should be able to see its purpose.
- From time to time, rules should be examined to see if they still make sense.
  (NB - this provides an opportunity to examine existing classroom rules.)

Project

Other ideas that can be substituted for any one or more of the above items, or used as follow-up activities/homework.

There is a concern that young people are buying and watching videos and video games containing violence unsuitable for their age. What rules could you devise to stop this from happening? (Note: this question is better suited to older pupils.)

A group of people sail away to an island to start a new life. They soon find that no-one wants to do the hard work needed to grow food and build houses. Do a CAF on this situation using Yellow, Black and Red Cap Thinking, and then invent some rules using White and Green Cap Thinking.

Practising Using Rules – Lesson 4, Worksheet 12

School Rules

Our chosen rule is:

_____

_____

Do a full CAF and remember [   ]

Yellow Cap - What are the advantages or benefits of the rule?

_____

_____

Black Cap - What are the weaknesses/dangers/problems with the rule?

_____

_____

Red Cap - What/how do I feel about the rule?

_____

_____

How will the rule affect our class?

_____

_____

How will the rule affect other classes?

_____

_____

How will the rule affect the whole school?

_____

_____

After 5 minutes we will compare answers.

Practising Using Rules – Lesson 4, Worksheet 13

Parents' Rules for Managing Children

Our chosen rule is:

P

_____

_____

_____

_____

M

_____

_____

_____

_____

_____

I

_____

_____

_____

_____

_____

After 5 minutes we will compare answers.

Lesson 5

Consequences and Sequel: C&S

(Part 1)

General introduction (5 minutes)	Explain what we mean by C&S then explain the difference between C&S and CAF
Group activity (15 minutes)	Use a PMI to look at the difference between electric and steam engines.
Introduction	Time scales (5 minutes).
Group activity (15 minutes)	Practising using time scales.
(10 minutes)	Practising risk-versus certainty.
Resources	Worksheets 14-17.
	Lesson Posters.pdf, page 4.

Introduction

What is C&S?

Teacher:

C&S stands for Consequences and Sequel.

It is the process of looking ahead to see the consequences of an action, a plan, a decision, a rule or an invention.

The difference between C&S and CAF is...

CAF	C&S
Factors operating at the moment on which decisions are based.	What may happen after the decision has been made.
Thinking about a situation at the moment.	Thinking ahead and focusing directly on the future.

Teacher:

C&S is concerned with an action that we intend to take or an action that others are taking. An action may seem worthwhile if the immediate effect is good but, when we make an effort to look at the longer-term consequences, the action may not seem worthwhile after all. Conversely, an action that has good long-term consequences may not seem very enticing at the moment.

Example

The invention of the petrol engine made possible cars, buses, lorries and aeroplanes together with a great deal of pollution.

If all the consequences could have been foreseen at the time, electric or steam engines might have been more commonly used.

At this point ask the whole class to complete Worksheet 14 to prompt a PMI discussion for electric and steam engines and list responses. Allow 5 minutes for pupils to complete the Worksheet and 10 minutes for feedback.

The main principle is that:

New inventions, plans, rules or decisions all have consequences that go on for a long time. In thinking about actions, consequences should always be considered.

Time Scale

Immediate: The immediate consequences of the action.

Short-term: What happens after the immediate consequences?

Medium-term: What happens when things have settled down?

Long-term: What happens much later?

Example

A man introduced rabbits to Australia to provide hunting for his friends.

Immediate consequences: Good - the man's friends have plenty of rabbits to shoot at.

Short-term consequences: Good - the rabbit is an alternative source of meat/food.

Medium-term consequences: Bad - the rabbits multiplied and became pests.

Long-term consequences: Very bad - the rabbit damaged crops.

Group Activity

Practise using time-scales

> **With increasing automation it is possible that in the future people will need to work only three hours a day.**

Divide the class into 4 groups and ask each group to nominate a spokesperson to feedback to the whole class using Worksheet 15. Ask one group to look at the immediate consequences, another group to look at short-term consequences, a third group to look at medium-term consequences and a fourth group to look at long-term consequences. Allow the groups 5 minutes to complete this activity and 10 minutes feedback time.

Practise using risk and certainty

> **A new medicine is discovered that will allow people to live to the age of 120 years, but the medicine is very expensive.**

Divide the class into groups of 4 -6 pupils and nominate one pupil from each group to be a spokesperson to feedback to the whole class using notes from Worksheets 16 and 17. Ask half the groups to try and identify the risks involved by making suggestions for answers to the questions above, and ask the other half to identify any certainties associated with this idea from the list above (allow 5 minutes for this activity).

Choose two pupils - one from each half of the class - to present their suggestions/arguments to the whole class. Allow 2 minutes for each presentation. At the end of the presentations, invite the class to vote for the most convincing presentation / argument.

Consequences and Sequel – Lesson 5, Worksheet 14

Electric engines

P

_____

_____

_____

_____

_____

M

_____

_____

_____

_____

_____

I

_____

_____

_____

_____

_____

Steam engines

P

_____

_____

_____

_____

_____

M

_____

_____

_____

_____

_____

I

_____

_____

_____

_____

_____

Practising C&S – Lesson 5, Worksheet 15

Consequences and Sequel

With increasing automation it is possible that in the future people will need to work only three hours a day. What are the:

Immediate consequences?

_____

_____

_____

_____

Short-term consequences (1-5 years)?

_____

_____

_____

_____

Medium-term consequences (5-10 years)?

_____

_____

_____

_____

Long-term consequences (10+ years)?

_____

_____

_____

_____

We will compare answers after 5 minutes.

Practising Risk versus Certainty – Lesson 5, Worksheet 16

Consequences and Sequel: Risks

A new medicine is discovered that will allow people to live to the age of 120 years, but the medicine is very expensive.

Will it work?

_____

_____

_____

What is the worst thing that could happen?

_____

_____

_____

What are the actual dangers?

_____

_____

_____

What is the best thing that could happen?

_____

_____

_____

What is most likely to happen?

_____

_____

_____

Are the consequences reversible?

_____

After 5 minutes you will present your answers to the whole class.

Practising Risk versus Certainty – Lesson 5, Worksheet 17

Consequences and Sequel: Certainty

A new medicine is discovered that will allow people to live to the age of 120 years but the medicine is very expensive.

Why do you think the medicine will work?

_____

_____

_____

_____

What is most likely to happen as a result of people taking the medicine?

_____

_____

_____

_____

What are you not sure about?

_____

_____

_____

_____

Why can't you be sure about what will happen?

_____

_____

_____

_____

After 5 minutes you will present your answers to the whole class.

Lesson 6

Consequences and Sequel: C&S

(Part 2)

Introduction
(5 minutes)

Recapitulate what is meant by C&S.

Group activity
(40 minutes)

Practising using C&S.

Process
(5 minutes)

Discuss the process involved in using C&S.

Principles
(5 minutes)

Describe the principles of C&S.

Project
(optional)

Use any one or more of the practice items and/or additional items for homework.

Resources

Worksheets 18-21.

Lesson Posters.pdf, page 4.

Introduction

What is C&S?

Teacher:

C&S stands for Consequences and Sequel.

It is the process of looking ahead to see the consequences of an action, a plan, a decision, a rule or an invention.

Practising using C&S

> **A new law is suggested to allow children to leave school and to start earning money as soon as they want to after the age of 12 years.**

Do a C&S on this from the point of view of:

- someone who leaves school early
- schools
- the local community and/or society in general.

Divide the class into groups of 4-6 pupils with a nominated spokesperson for feedback. Use Worksheet 18 so that each group tackles one of the above.

(Note - more than one group can tackle each of the above situations.) Encourage each group to do the C&S from immediate, short-term, medium-term and long-term point of view.

At the end of 5 minutes, feedback is invited from each point of view via the designated groups. Allow 5 minutes for feedback.

Suggestions

- Children who don't like school will leave early and make lots of money. If they are successful they will not regret it but if unsuccessful they might.
- There might be pressure from parents to make children leave school early.
- Schools might benefit because the children remaining at school really want to be there and want to work.
- The children who leave school early might not find it easy to find jobs.
- The children who leave early and don't get a job might be a problem for the community.
- Society might suffer with wide differences amongst its members.

> **Some research shows that watching television for hours on end is bad for the brain. Do a C&S on this.**

Divide the class into groups of 4-6 pupils with a nominated spokesperson in each group. Ask each group to respond to the research findings by doing a different time-scale C&S, using Worksheet 19.

(Note - more than one group can tackle each of the different time scales.)

Allow 5 minutes for this activity and then list the groups' responses. Ask the groups to nominate the consequences that seem to have the greatest/least certainty and the most/least risk. Allow 5 minutes for this feedback.

> **What are the consequences of arguing with your parents?**

Divide the class into groups of 4-6 pupils with a nominated spokesperson in each group, using Worksheet 20.

Ask each group to do a full C&S by using selected questions from Yellow, Black and Red Cap Thinking.

The time allowed for this activity is 5 minutes. Also take 5 minutes feedback time.

(Prompt - check to see if the immediate and long-term consequences are different/opposite to one another.)

> **A new device makes it possible to tell whenever someone is telling a lie. Do an immediate C&S on this.**

Divide the class into groups of 4-6 pupils with a nominated spokesperson in each group. Five minutes is allowed for the groups to consider this practice item, using Worksheet 21.

At the end of 5 minutes take one suggestion from each group until no more are forthcoming. Allow 5 minutes for feedback.

(Prompt - clues/suggestions relate to legal procedures, police interviewing suspected criminals, impact on peoples' behaviour - crime reduction, where would it be used? E.g. schools!)

Process

Teacher: C&S is the most important of all thinking tools in real life when thinking is going to result in taking some future action of any sort relating to decisions, choices, plans, etc. Looking at the consequences of actions means asking questions such as:

- Will it work? (Black Cap Thinking.)
- What are the benefits? (Yellow Cap Thinking.)
- What are the problems, dangers or risks? (Black Cap Thinking.)
- What are the costs? (Yellow Cap Thinking.)

What happens in the future affects other people as well as ourselves and something we do may put us in a better or worse 'position' to do something else.

Principles

- Others may be able to see the consequences of our actions more easily than we do.
- It is important to know whether the consequences are reversible or not.
- The immediate consequences and the long-term consequences may be opposite to one another.

▬ We should look at the consequences, not only as they affect us, but also as they affect others.

Project

Other ideas that can be substituted for any one or more of the above items or used as follow-up activities/homework.

Some new medical evidence suggests that people who are slightly overweight are healthier than people who are underweight. What consequences do you think this will have? Do a full C&S.

What would happen if there was a method for teaching dogs to speak? Do an immediate consequences on this.

Practising using C&S – Lesson 6, Worksheet 18

Consequences and Sequel

A new law is suggested to allow children to leave school and start earning money as soon as they want to after the age of 12 years.

Do a C&S on this from the point of view of one of the following:

☐ someone who leaves school early

☐ schools

☐ the local community and/or society in general.

Please put a tick alongside the one chosen.

The immediate consequences are:

_____

_____

_____

The short-term consequences (1-5 years) are:

_____

_____

_____

The medium-term consequences (5-10 years) are:

_____

_____

_____

The long-term consequences (10+ years) are:

_____

_____

_____

After 5 minutes we will compare answers.

Practising using C&S – Lesson 6, Worksheet 19

Consequences and Sequel

Some research shows that watching television for hours on end is bad for the brain. Make clear which consequence your group has been asked to work on, and do a C&S

Immediate:

_____

_____

_____

Short-term (1-5 years):

_____

_____

_____

Medium-term (5-10 years):

_____

_____

_____

Long-term (10+ years):

_____

_____

_____

Our group discussed:

_____

_____

_____

_____ consequences.

After 5 minutes we will compare answers.

Practising using C&S – Lesson 6, Worksheet 20

Consequences and Sequel

What are the consequences of arguing with your parents?

Do a full C&S and remember…

Yellow Cap - What are the advantages/benefits of arguing with your parents?

_____

_____

Black Cap - What are the weaknesses/dangers/problems with arguing?

_____

_____

Red Cap - What/how do I feel about arguing with my parents?

_____

_____

What are the immediate consequences of arguing with my parents?

_____

What are the short-term consequences (1-2 days)?

_____

What are the medium-term consequences (2-7 days)?

_____

What are the long-term consequences (1-4 weeks)?

_____

After 5 minutes we will compare answers.

Practising using C&S – Lesson 6, Worksheet 21

Consequences and Sequel

A new device makes it possible to tell whenever someone is telling a lie.

Do an immediate C&S on this.

After 5 minutes we will compare answers.

Lesson 7
Aims, Goals and Objectives: AGO

Introduction
(10 minutes)

Explain what is meant by AGO (contains a group activity).

Group activity
(35 minutes)

Practising using AGO.

Process
(5 minutes)

Describe the process involved in using AGO.

Principles
(10 minutes)

Describe the principles of AGO (contains a group activity).

Project
(optional)

Use any one or more of the practice items and/or additional items for homework.

Resources

Worksheets 22-29.

Lesson Posters.pdf, page 5.

Introduction

What is AGO?

Teacher:

AGO stands for Aims, Goals and Objectives.

We can do something:

- out of habit
- because everyone else is doing it
- as a reaction to a situation.

These are all 'because' reasons.

There are times when we intend or try to do something and these are often referred to as Aims. There are also times when we do something in order to achieve some purpose or Objective. The object of our efforts is often described as ambition or Goal.

It can help our thinking if we know exactly what we are trying to achieve and it can help us to understand other people's thinking if we can see their Aims, Goals or Objectives.

Example

Ask the whole class what Aims, Goals or Objectives a developer building a large new shopping centre might have.

Suggestions (NB - not necessarily the correct or only answers):

- making a profit
- building a successful centre
- pleasing shoppers
- fitting in with the planning authority
- completing work on time to get more business.

Note also: For the purpose of the practice items that follow, Aims, Goals and Objectives can be used interchangeably.

Group Activity

Practising using AGO

1   What would your objectives be if you won £5 million on the lottery?

2   What are the objectives of school tests?

3   What are your objectives when you turn on the TV?

4   What are the objectives of a headteacher?

Divide the class into 8 groups and number them 1-8. Give each group the appropriate Worksheets, 22-29. (Note: this is a parallel activity – Worksheets 22 and 26 relate to question 1 above, Worksheets 23 and 27 relate to question 2 above etc.)

Allow them 5 minutes to record their objectives on the Worksheet. After 5 minutes the sheets are passed onto the next group to add to the recorded suggestions and continue this process twice more so that after 20 minutes each group should have their original sheet back for feedback to the whole class.

Allow 10 minutes feedback time by taking one or two responses each time from a different group until no more different responses are forthcoming. (Note - you can compare the similarities and differences between groups 1-4 and groups 5-8.)

Ask each group to record the two most important objectives - give them 2 minutes thinking time and allow 3 minutes feedback time to the whole class.

(Note - you can compare the similarities and differences between groups 1-4 and groups 5-8.)

Process

This is another attention-directing tool.

It is related to the thinking habit of wanting to know the focus and purpose of thinking at every moment. However, AGO is more concerned with the overall purpose or objective of the thinking (Blue Cap Thinking) than the moment-to-moment thinking.

Principles

■ If we know exactly what our objectives are it is easier to achieve them.

Prompt: Ask the whole class for some examples.

■ In the same situation different people may have different objectives.

Prompt: Give examples of any different objectives you and your class may have.

Project

Other ideas that can be substituted for any one or more of the above items or used as follow-up activities/homework.

■ Do an AGO for the police and put the objectives in order of priority.

■ You are the commander of a spacecraft approaching Earth from another planet. What objectives might you have?

■ You think that the clothes your friend is wearing do not suit her/him. What would be your objectives in confronting her/him with your views?

■ What are your personal objectives for going to school? What do you think are the objectives of your parents, teachers and society in general for children and young people going to school?

■ There is a scare that certain tinned foods from a particular manufacturing company contain some harmful substances. This has not been proved. If you were the head of that company what would your AGO be?

Aims, Goals and Objectives

Group number: 1

What would be your objectives if you won £5 million on the lottery?

Group 1 comments:

_____

_____

_____

_____

_____

_____

Group 2 comments:

_____

_____

_____

_____

_____

_____

Group 3 comments:

_____

_____

_____

_____

_____

_____

Group 4 comments:

_____

_____

_____

_____

_____

_____

The two most important objectives are: (to be completed after this sheet is returned - that is, after 20 minutes)

1 _____

2 _____

After 5 minutes pass this onto the next group.

Practising using AGO – Lesson 7, Worksheet 23

Aims, Goals and Objectives

Group number: 2

What are the objectives of school tests?

Group 1 comments:

_____

_____

_____

_____

_____

_____

Group 2 comments:

_____

_____

_____

_____

_____

_____

Group 3 comments:

_____

_____

_____

_____

_____

_____

Group 4 comments:

_____

_____

_____

_____

_____

_____

The two most important objectives are: (to be completed after this sheet is returned - that is, after 20 minutes)

1 _____

2 _____

After 5 minutes pass this onto the next group.

Practising using AGO – Lesson 7, Worksheet 24

Aims, Goals and Objectives

Group number: 3

What are your objectives when you turn on the TV?

Group 1 comments:

_____

_____

_____

_____

_____

Group 2 comments:

_____

_____

_____

_____

_____

Group 3 comments:

_____

_____

_____

_____

_____

Group 4 comments:

_____

_____

_____

_____

_____

The two most important objectives are: (to be completed after this sheet is returned - that is, after 20 minutes)

1 _____

2 _____

After 5 minutes pass this onto the next group.

Practising using AGO – Lesson 7, Worksheet 25

Aims, Goals and Objectives

Group number: 4

What are the objectives of a headteacher?

Group 1 comments:

_____

_____

_____

_____

_____

Group 2 comments:

_____

_____

_____

_____

_____

Group 3 comments:

_____

_____

_____

_____

_____

Group 4 comments:

_____

_____

_____

_____

_____

The two most important objectives are: (to be completed after this sheet is returned - that is, after 20 minutes)

1 _____

2 _____

After 5 minutes pass this onto the next group.

Practising using AGO – Lesson 7, Worksheet 26

Aims, Goals and Objectives

Group number: 5

What would your objectives be if you won £5 million on the lottery?

Group 5 comments: Group 6 comments:

_____   _____

_____   _____

_____   _____

_____   _____

_____   _____

Group 7 comments: Group 8 comments:

_____   _____

_____   _____

_____   _____

_____   _____

_____   _____

The two most important objectives are: (to be completed after this sheet is returned - that is, after 20 minutes)

1 _____

2 _____

After 5 minutes pass this onto the next group.

Practising using AGO – Lesson 7, Worksheet 27

Aims, Goals and Objectives

Group number: 6

What are the objectives of school tests?

Group 5 comments:

_____

_____

_____

_____

_____

Group 6 comments:

_____

_____

_____

_____

_____

Group 7 comments:

_____

_____

_____

_____

_____

Group 8 comments:

_____

_____

_____

_____

_____

The two most important objectives are: (to be completed after this sheet is returned - that is, after 20 minutes)

1 _____

2 _____

After 5 minutes pass this onto the next group.

Practising using AGO – Lesson 7, Worksheet 28

Aims, Goals and Objectives

Group number: 7

What are your objectives when you turn on the TV?

Group 5 comments:

_____

_____

_____

_____

_____

Group 6 comments:

_____

_____

_____

_____

_____

Group 7 comments:

_____

_____

_____

_____

_____

Group 8 comments:

_____

_____

_____

_____

_____

The two most important objectives are: (to be completed after this sheet is returned - that is, after 20 minutes)

1 _____

2 _____

After 5 minutes pass this onto the next group.

Practising using AGO – Lesson 7, Worksheet 29

Aims, Goals and Objectives

Group number: 8

What are the objectives of a headteacher?

Group 5 comments:

_____

_____

_____

_____

_____

Group 6 comments:

_____

_____

_____

_____

_____

Group 7 comments:

_____

_____

_____

_____

_____

Group 8 comments:

_____

_____

_____

_____

_____

The two most important objectives are: (to be completed after this sheet is returned - that is, after 20 minutes)

1 _____

2 _____

After 5 minutes pass this onto the next group.

Lesson 8
Planning

Introduction
(10 minutes)

Explain what is meant by planning (contains a group activity).

Group activity
(35 minutes)

Practising using planning.

Process
(5 minutes)

Describe the process behind planning.

Principles
(10 minutes)

Describe the principles of planning (contains a group activity).

Project
(optional)

Use any one or more of the practice items and/or additional items for homework.

Resources

Worksheets 30-34.

Lesson Posters.pdf, page 6.

Introduction

What is planning?

Teacher:

Planning is thinking ahead to see how you are going to do something.

It may be a matter of:

- getting somewhere
- getting something done
- organising things so they run smoothly.

Example

Ask the class:

Can you think of some examples of plans that either you have made or need to make, or plans that adults have made for you?

Prompts: What are you going to do when you get home this evening?

What TV programmes are you going to watch?

What are you going to do over the weekend/next school holiday?

What homework are you going to do and in which order?

Which relatives are you going to visit?

Group Activity

Practising Planning

> **You get permission to arrange a school disco on a Saturday evening but only if you can come up with a suitable plan.**

Divide the class into six groups. Ask two groups to do a CAF on this idea (see Worksheet 30). Ask another two groups to do a C&S on this idea (see Worksheet 31). Ask the third pair of groups to do an AGO on this idea (see Worksheet 32).

Ask each group to nominate a spokesperson to feedback the group's responses from the wWorksheets. Allow 5 minutes for recording ideas.

After 5 minutes take responses from each group in turn and record the answers on a board. (Note the similarities and differences between the parallel groups.) Take responses from the class as each group presents their ideas until no more responses are forthcoming.

Allow 10 minutes for feedback. After 10 minutes ask each group to record their plan (on Worksheet 33) and remind the groups to take account of CAF, C&S and AGO.

Allow 5 minutes for recording plans and take one response from each group at a time until no more responses are forthcoming. (Note the similarities and differences between the parallel groups.) Allow 5 minutes feedback time.

> Your objective is to make money and you have the choice of any three
> of the following:
>
> - 5 mountain bikes
> - a horse
> - 2,000 old books and magazines
> - 200 large tins of red paint
> - a printing machine
> - a new recipe for pizzas.
>
> Make a plan showing how you would use your choice of three things.

Divide the class into 6 groups. Ask each group to nominate a spokesperson to
feedback the group's responses from Worksheet 34. Allow 5 minutes for recording
ideas.

Take each group's choice of three items and ask each group to give the reasons for
their choices. Comment on similarity and differences. Take a plan from one group.
Allow 5 minutes for feedback.

Process

Discuss the following questions with the class:

━ What is difficult about planning?

Prompt: It may not always be possible to foresee all the factors involved and/or the
consequences of the plan.

━ When are plans necessary?

Prompt: When some future action or project is proposed, or as a means of graphical
representation - ground plan.

━ What is the most important thing about planning?

Prompt: To know what you want to achieve in the end.

━ What are the disadvantages of planning?

Prompt: It can prevent spontaneity and/or creativity.

Principles

━ In planning, it is important to know exactly what you want to achieve (AGO).

━ Always have an alternative plan ready in case something goes wrong with the
  first plan.

━ The value of a plan depends upon its consequences (C&S).

Project

Other ideas that can be substituted for any one or more of the above items or used as follow-up activities/homework.

> **The centre of a town has become a slum and the council wants to do something about it. Do a CAF and AGO for the council.**

What plan should they make? Put the plan in three stages.

— Do a C&S on the plan.

— Devise a plan that would make it easier for people to find jobs they liked.

— A thief has been stealing people's money and belongings from a swimming pool. How would you plan to catch this thief?

Practising Planning – Lesson 8, Worksheet 30

Planning

You get permission to arrange a school disco on a Saturday evening but only if you can come up with a suitable plan.

Do a CAF for arranging the disco first.

Remember to consider:

Factors affecting pupils/students:

_____

_____

_____

_____

_____

Factors affecting teachers:

_____

_____

_____

_____

_____

Factors affecting parents:

_____

_____

_____

_____

_____

After 5 minutes we will discuss this with the rest of the class.

Practising Planning – Lesson 8, Worksheet 31

Planning

You get permission to arrange a school disco on a Saturday evening but only if you can come up with a suitable plan.

Do a C&S for arranging the disco first.

Remember:

Yellow Cap Thinking - What are the advantages/benefits of the disco?

_____

_____

Black Cap Thinking - What are dangers or problems with organising a disco?

_____

_____

Red Cap Thinking - How do I feel about organising a disco?

_____

_____

What are the immediate consequences of organising a disco?

_____

_____

What are the short-term consequences (1-2 days)?

_____

_____

What are the medium-term consequences (up to 1 week)?

_____

_____

What are the long-term consequences (up to 4 weeks)?

_____

_____

After 5 minutes we will discuss this with the rest of the class.

Practising Planning – Lesson 8, Worksheet 32

Planning

You get permission to arrange a school disco on a Saturday evening but only if you can come up with a suitable plan.

Do an AGO for arranging the disco first.

_____

_____

_____

_____

_____

_____

_____

_____

_____

_____

_____

The four most important objectives are:

1 _____

2 _____

3 _____

4 _____

After 5 minutes we will discuss this with the rest of the class.

Practising Planning – Lesson 8, Worksheet 33

Planning

You get permission to arrange a school disco on a Saturday evening but only if you can come up with a suitable plan.

Remember to take into account all the factors involved (CAF), the consequences (C&S) and your objectives (AGO).

_____

_____

_____

_____

_____

_____

_____

_____

_____

_____

_____

_____

_____

_____

_____

_____

_____

_____

After 5 minutes we will discuss this with the rest of the class.

Practising Planning – Lesson 8, Worksheet 34

Planning

Your objective is to make money and you have the choice of any three of the following:

- 5 mountain bikes
- a horse
- 2,000 old books and magazines
- 200 large tins of red paint
- a printing machine
- a new recipe for pizzas.

Make a plan showing how you would use your choice of three things.

Our three choices are:

1 _____

2 _____

3 _____

Our plan to make money is:

_____

_____

_____

_____

_____

_____

_____

_____

_____

After 5 minutes we will discuss this with the rest of the class.

Lesson 9
First Important Priorities: FIP

Introduction
(5 minutes)

Explain what is meant by FIP.

Group activity
(45 minutes)

Practising using FIP.

Process
(5 minutes)

Describe the process behind FIP.

Principles
(5 minutes)

Describe the principles of FIP.

Project
(optional)

Use any one or more of the practice items and/or additional items for homework.

Resources

Worksheets 35-37.

Lesson Posters.pdf, page 7.

Introduction

What is FIP?

Teacher:

FIP stands for First Important Priorities.

- Some things are more important than others.
- Some factors are more important than others.
- Some objectives are more important than others.
- Some consequences are more important than others.

In thinking about a situation after we have got a lot of ideas, we have to decide which ones are more important so that we can do something about them.

After doing a PMI, CAF, C&S or AGO we can do a FIP to pick out the most important points and deal with them first.

Example

Teacher:

Someone wants to borrow some money from you.

— What factors would you consider?

— What are the priorities?

Suggestions

— Do you have the money?

— Do you trust the borrower?

— Can you afford to lend the money?

— When will the borrower pay back the money?

Group Activity

Practising using FIP

What makes a television programme interesting?

Do a CAF and then a FIP.

Divide the class into six groups. Ask each group to list about 6 factors and then pick out a top 3 - tell the groups that these factors need not be given in order of importance.

After 5 minutes the nominated spokesperson for each group is asked to give one response at a time from Worksheet 35. This process is repeated until no further ideas are forthcoming. Allow 10 minutes in total for feedback.

> **Do a FIP on choosing a friend.**

Keep the class in their six groups. Ask each group to work on the problem for 5 minutes using Worksheet 36. After 5 minutes ask one group to give its output via the nominated person and write the responses on a board. Ask other groups to say whether they agree or disagree and ask them to give a brief reason. After one group has given its responses and other groups have agreed/disagreed, different responses can be added to the list. Allow 10 minutes for feedback.

> **Do an AGO and then a FIP on running an effective school.**

Keep the class in their six groups. Ask each group to do an AGO followed by a FIP for 5 minutes using Worksheet 37. Ask one group to give all its objectives via the nominated person and then ask another to give its top three priorities. Ask for comments from the other groups.

Allow 10 minutes for feedback.

Suggestions

- for better examination results
- for better behaviour
- for good attendance
- for helping in the community
- for good pupil-pupil and pupil-staff relationships.

Process

- FIP is an attention-directing thinking tool related to AGO.
- FIP allows both parallel thinking and narrowing down or 'focusing in' (Blue Cap Thinking).
- FIP is concerned directly with priorities such as safety, human rights and justice, law and order, costs etc.
- Some priorities, such as pollution, have to be avoided.

Principles

- It is important to get as many ideas as possible first and then start picking out priorities.
- Different people can have different priorities in the same situation.
- We should know exactly why we have chosen something as a priority.

Project

Other ideas that can be substituted for any one or more of the above items or used as follow-up activities/homework.

- If you were choosing people to be good police officers, what would be your top three priorities?

- When a child or young person has done something wrong, what would be the three top priorities of their parents?

- What would be the three priorities for parents and children/young people in arranging the time that children/young people should return home after an evening out with friends? (Choose ages of children/young people to suit.)

Practising using FIP – Lesson 9, Worksheet 35

First Important Priorities

What makes a television programme interesting?

Do a CAF and then a FIP. Remember to consider:

Factors about yourself:

_____

_____

_____

_____

Factors about others who will want to watch the television:

_____

_____

_____

_____

Factors about society in general:

_____

_____

_____

The three most important factors are:

_____

_____

_____

After 5 minutes we will discuss this with the rest of the class.

Practising using FIP – Lesson 9, Worksheet 36

First Important Priorities

Do a FIP on choosing a friend.

Remember to list all the factors and objectives before deciding what are the most important...

Factors:

_____

_____

_____

_____

_____

Objectives:

_____

_____

_____

_____

_____

FIP:

_____

_____

_____

_____

_____

After 5 minutes we will discuss this with the rest of the class.

Practising using FIP – Lesson 9, Worksheet 37

First Important Priorities

Do an AGO and then a FIP for running a school.

Objectives (remember some key questions - Blue Cap Thinking).

What is the purpose of school?

_____

_____

_____

_____

What makes schools effective?

_____

_____

_____

_____

What do others (parents, teachers, the community/society) think about the purpose of school and what makes schools effective?

_____

_____

_____

_____

FIP:

_____

_____

_____

After 5 minutes we will discuss this with the rest of the class.

Lesson 10
Alternatives, Possibilities, Choices: APC

Introduction
(5 minutes)

Explain what is meant by APC.

Group activity
(40 minutes)

Practising using APC.

Process
(5 minutes)

Describe the process behind APC.

Principles
(5 minutes)

Describe the principles of APC.

Project
(optional)

Use any one or more of the practice items and/or additional items for homework.

Resources

Worksheets 38-40.

Lesson Posters.pdf, page 8.

Introduction

What is APC?

Teacher:

APC stands for Alternatives, Possibilities, Choices.

When making choices or taking action, we may find that there are more alternatives than we first thought. In looking at situations, there may also be other possible explanations that we had not thought of.

Example

A crashed car is found in a ditch and the driver is dead. What could have happened?

Suggestions

- The driver had a heart attack or fainted.
- The car had a puncture or broke down.
- The driver was drunk.
- The driver had misjudged the bend in the road.
- The driver was attacked by a bee or wasp and lost concentration.
- The driver fell asleep.
- The driver had been murdered and then placed in the crashed car.

Group Activity

Practising using ACP

> **A woman goes into a café and asks for a drink of water. The person at the counter gives her a drink of water, then suddenly screams! What are the possible explanations?**

Explain that you have a possible explanation (see prompt below).

Ask the whole class to suggest possible explanations and list them.

Allow 5 minutes.

Prompt

The woman asked for a glass of water because she was hiccupping and the person behind the counter in the café knew that hiccups can often be cured by a sudden fright, so she screamed to frighten the woman.

> **You discover that your best friend is a thief at school. What alternatives do you have?**

Divide the class into six groups. Ask each group to list the alternatives on Worksheet 38. After 5 minutes ask the nominated spokesperson for each group to give one response at a time and record these on the board. This process is repeated until no further ideas are forthcoming - also see prompts below. Allow 10 minutes in total for feedback.

Suggestions

- Tell your friend you know that s/he is a thief.
- Threaten to report your friend to a member of staff, your class teacher or the head teacher.
- Report your friend to a member of staff, your class teacher or the head teacher.
- Drop her/him as a friend after explaining why.
- Drop her/him as a friend without explaining why.
- Tell your friend how much you hate stealing without 'letting on' that you know s/he is a thief.
- Get someone else to talk to your friend.
- Leave a note for your friend saying one or more of the above.

> **A man is seen walking in a shopping centre with a brown paper bag over his head. Do an APC and list at least 5 possible explanations.**

Ask the class to get back into their six groups. Ask each group to list at least five possible alternatives on Worksheet 39. After 5 minutes ask the nominated spokesperson for each group to give one response at a time and record these on the board. This process is repeated until no further ideas are forthcoming. Allow 5 minutes for feedback.

> **Can you think of an alternative shape for a television screen? Use Yellow Cap Thinking to show the benefits of your new shape.**

Keep the class in their same groups. Ask each group to list at least five possible alternatives and benefits on Worksheet 40. After 5 minutes ask the nominated spokesperson for each group to give one response at a time and record these on the board. This process is repeated until no further ideas are forthcoming. Allow 5 minutes for feedback.

Process

- APC is another attention-directing thinking tool but instead of moving forward we look at parallel possibilities.
- Green Cap Thinking is used for finding alternatives (or solutions) and Yellow Cap Thinking can be used to identify the 'benefits' of these alternatives or solutions.
- The more humour is used, the more creative and inventive our thinking can be.
- There can be many kinds of alternatives, possibilities or choices. Some involve perception, some involve action, some are linked with approaches, some offer explanations and some are related to design.

■ Some alternatives, possibilities and choices are forced upon us, whilst there are others that we can look for.

Principles

■ If you cannot think of any alternatives yourself, you should ask someone else.

■ You should go on looking for alternatives until you find one that you really like.

■ There is almost always an alternative, even if there does not appear to be one at first.

■ You cannot know that the obvious explanation is best until you have looked at some other alternative explanations.

■ To look for alternatives when you are not satisfied is easy, but to look for alternatives when you are satisfied requires a deliberate effort.

Project

Other ideas that can be substituted for any one or more of the above items or used as follow-up activities/homework.

■ The brightest pupil/student in a class starts making mistakes with her/his work on purpose. What possible explanations are there?

■ An object is described as round, flat and delicious to eat in a TV quiz show. Other than a burger, what else could this object be?

■ Some areas around school/where you live are very dirty because people drop litter and empty cans everywhere. How would you suggest tackling this problem?

■ Plan an alternative classroom for the future and list the benefits for teachers and pupils/students.

Practising using APC – Lesson 10, Worksheet 38

Alternatives, Possibilities, Choices

You discover that your best friend is a thief at school. What alternatives do you have?

Remember, finding alternatives is about using Green Cap Thinking so you should be looking for solutions as well as alternatives.

_____

_____

_____

_____

_____

_____

_____

_____

_____

_____

_____

_____

Our preferred solution is:

_____

_____

_____

_____

After 5 minutes we will discuss this with the rest of the class.

Practising using APC – Lesson 10, Worksheet 39

Alternatives, Possibilities, Choices

A man is seen walking in a shopping centre with a brown paper bag over his head. Do an APC and list at least 5 possible explanations.

Remember, Green Cap Thinking is being used so you should try and be creative and inventive with your choices of explanation.

After 5 minutes we will discuss this with the rest of the class.

Practising using APC – Lesson 10, Worksheet 40

Alternatives, Possibilities, Choices

Can you think of an alternative shape for a television screen?

Remember to use Green Cap Thinking for creative and inventive alternatives.

_____

_____

_____

_____

_____

_____

_____

Remember to use Yellow Cap Thinking to show the benefits of your new television shape.

_____

_____

_____

_____

_____

_____

After 5 minutes we will discuss this with the rest of the class.

Lesson 11
Decisions

Introduction
(10 minutes)

Explain why decision making is important.

Group activity
(40 minutes)

Practising decision making.

Process
(5 minutes)

Describe the process behind decision making.

Principles
(5 minutes)

Describe the principles of decision making.

Project
(optional)

Use any one or more of the practice items and/or additional items for homework.

Resources

Worksheets 41-43.
A4 Paper.

Lesson Posters.pdf, page 9.

Introduction

Why decision making is important

Teacher:

Some decisions are easy and some are difficult. How easy or difficult a decision might be depends on the person and the situation.

There are decisions that need to be made all the time, such as:

- What clothes to wear?
- What records to buy?
- Whether to go out or stay in?
- Whether to spend money or to save it?

Sometimes the decision is a choice between two alternatives such as whether to spend money or to save it. Sometimes the decision is forced on you such as having to go left or right at a T junction.

In making decisions it is useful to be clear about the:

- factors involved (CAF)
- objectives (AGO)
- priorities (FIP)
- consequences (C&S)
- alternatives (APC).

Group Activity

Practising making Decisions

> **A police officer notices a light on in a warehouse when she is on duty late at night. The warehouse is locked up and she is on her own. She knows that it is unusual for a light to be on. She has to make a quick decision as to what she is going to do next.**

Explain that you have 5 possible explanations (see prompt below). Ask the whole class to make suggestions and comment on the similarities and differences to yours.

Allow 10 minutes for suggestions, ask follow-up questions and record on the board any one or more suggestions not included in the prompt below:

Suggestions

▬ Stay where she is and radio for help.

▬ Radio for help and then go into the warehouse.

(You could then ask what she might do if she discovered that the radio wasn't working and this may prompt other suggestions from the class.)

▬ Try and get closer to see how many people are involved.

▬ If only one, she could make an arrest.

(You could ask what factors might be involved in deciding whether she should try and get closer.)

▬ Wait outside and then follow the person/people who come out.

(You could ask what factors might be involved in deciding whether to wait and follow.)

▬ Look for a possible getaway car parked nearby and let down the tyres.

(You could ask what factors might be involved in deciding whether to look for a possible getaway car and let down the tyres.)

Decide why people like advertising.

Divide the class into six groups. Ask two groups to do a CAF on this using Worksheet 41. Ask another two groups to do an AGO and a FIP on this using Worksheet 42. Ask another two groups to do a C&S on this using Worksheet 43.

After 5 minutes, ask the nominated spokesperson for each group to give their responses one at a time from her/his Worksheet and allow other groups to add ideas. (Note the similarities and differences between the two groups using the same thinking tools - CAF, AGO and FIP, C&S.)

This process is repeated until no further ideas are forthcoming from any of the groups. Allow 10 minutes in total for feedback.

You meet an alien on the way home from school. He is so fed up with the human race that he has decided to wipe us out in 30 seconds time.

Decide what you would say to him to try and stop him.

Keep the pupils/students in their groups and ask them to generate as many ideas as possible (Green Cap Thinking) on a blank sheet of paper.

After 5 minutes ask the nominated person from the group with the most ideas to say them out loud and when s/he has finished, ask other groups to add any ideas that have not been said (allow 5 minutes for feedback).

Process

Discuss with the whole class the following questions:

▬ Why are some decisions easier than others?

Prompt: Because some decisions are a choice between two or more alternatives and some decisions are forced upon us.

▬ What are the most important things to think about when making a decision?

Prompt: the factors involved (CAF)

the objectives (AGO)

the priorities (FIP)

the consequences (C&S)

the alternatives (APC).

■ How can you tell that the decision you have made is the right one?

Prompt: The answers to the above should help.

■ Is it better to think about decisions or just to make them and see what happens?

Prompt: It's obviously better to think about decisions first because without doing so we may miss some important factors, alternatives or priorities. We may also fail to see whether decisions taken are reversible or not.

Principles

■ You should always be able to tell yourself the real reason behind any decision you make.

■ It is important to know whether or not a decision is reversible.

■ Not making a decision is really a decision to do nothing.

Project

Other ideas that can be substituted for any one or more of the above items or used as follow-up activities/homework.

■ You are offered £1,000 now or £5,000 in a year's time.

● How would you decide between the two?

● Explain the reasons behind your decisions.

● Do a C&S on both choices.

■ Decide what people would do if television hadn't been invented.

■ Decide on the reasons for why cars should be developed to go faster.

■ Decide what makes people happy.

Practising making Decisions – Lesson 11, Worksheet 41

Decisions

Decide why people like advertising. Do a CAF on this and remember that for CAF you need to ask: What are the benefits? (Yellow Cap Thinking).

For you:

_____

_____

For others:

_____

_____

For society:

_____

_____

What are the dangers (Black Cap Thinking)?

_____

_____

For you:

_____

_____

For others:

_____

_____

What do you feel about advertising (Red Cap Thinking)?

_____

_____

After 5 minutes we will discuss this with the rest of the class.

Practising making Decisions – Lesson 11, Worksheet 42

Decisions

Decide why people like advertising. Do an AGO and a FIP on this and remember some key questions (Blue Cap Thinking) you need to ask.

What is the purpose of advertising?

_____

_____

_____

What makes advertising effective?

_____

_____

_____

What do your friends, family and teachers think about advertising and what makes advertising effective?

_____

_____

_____

_____

_____

_____

What are the two most important priorities when advertising?

1 _____

2 _____

After 5 minutes we will discuss this with the rest of the class.

Practising making Decisions – Lesson 11, Worksheet 43

Decisions

Decide why people like advertising. Do a C&S on this and remember that for a C&S you need to ask...

What are the immediate consequences?

_____

_____

_____

_____

What are the short-term consequences (1-2 days)?

_____

_____

_____

_____

What are the medium-term consequences (up to 1 week)?

_____

_____

_____

_____

What are the long-term consequences (up to 4 weeks)?

_____

_____

_____

_____

After 5 minutes we will discuss this with the rest of the class.

Lesson 12
Other People's Views: OPV

Introduction (10 minutes)	Explain what is meant by OPV and why OPV is important.
Group activity (40 minutes)	Practising OPV.
Process (5 minutes)	Describe the process behind OPV.
Principles (5 minutes)	Describe the principles of OPV.
Project (optional)	Use any one or more of the practice items and/or additional items for homework.
Resources	Worksheets 44-46. Lesson Posters.pdf, page 10.

Introduction

What is meant by OPV and why OPV is important

Teacher:

OPV means Other People's Views.

Most thinking involves other people and what these other people think is just as much a part of the situation as the factors involved - the consequences, the objectives and the priorities. These other people may have a different viewpoint from us, although the situation may be the same.

In fact, all the thinking we do for ourselves, others may be doing for themselves, only differently.

Example

A salesperson trying to sell you a used sports car will probably tell you that:

- The engine is very powerful.
- The bodywork is in excellent condition.
- The car suits you.
- The car is good value for money.

Your point of view is to see:

- How much petrol the car uses.
- Whether the car has been in a crash.
- What the car feels like to drive and whether the seats are comfortable.
- How the price of the car compares to other sports cars.

Group Activity

Practising using OPV

> **A father forbids his 13 year old daughter to smoke.**
>
> **What is the father's point of view?**
>
> **What is the daughter's point of view?**

Divide the class into groups of 4-6. Ask each group to record both the father's and daughter's points of view (on Worksheet 44).

After 5 minutes, ask a nominated person from one group to give the father's point of view. Ask the nominated person from another group to give the daughter's point of view. Allow other groups and individuals to add to the suggestions offered (allow 5 minutes feedback time).

Suggestions

Father's point of view:

- Smoking is bad for his daughter's health.

- Smoking is a waste of money.

- Smoking would make her breath and clothes smell.

- Allowing his daughter to smoke would make other people think that he is not bringing his daughter up properly.

- His daughter is too young to think for herself as an adult.

Daughter's point of view:

- She only wants to try out smoking because all her friends smoke and she is afraid of being the odd one out.

- She wants to be able to make decisions for herself - sooner or later she will be able to smoke anyway.

- She cannot see the harm in smoking.

> **A boy refuses to obey his teacher in class. The teacher reports the boy to the head teacher who excludes him. The boy's parents object.**
>
> **What are the boy's viewpoints?**
>
> **What are the teacher's viewpoints?**
>
> **What are the head teacher's viewpoints?**
>
> **What are the viewpoints of the class?**

Divide the class into four groups. Ask each group to record one of the four viewpoints above on Worksheet 45.

Allow 5 minutes for this activity and then ask the nominated spokesperson for each group to give their responses in turn. Allow other groups and individuals to add comments. Use 5 minutes for feedback.

> **A girl likes to do her homework listening to loud music. She doesn't want to use earphones. Her parents and her brother like to work in peace and quiet. Do an OPV on this situation.**

Divide the class into six groups - Worksheet 46 is used for this activity. Ask two groups to record their responses from the girl's viewpoint. Ask another two groups to record their responses from the brother's viewpoint. Ask another two groups to record their responses from the parents' viewpoint.

Allow 5 minutes for this activity and then ask the nominated spokesperson for each group or pair of groups to give their responses in turn. (Note the similarities and differences between the pairs of groups.)

Allow other groups and individuals to add comments. Use 5 minutes in total for feedback.

Process

Teacher:

This is another attention-directing tool.

There are two key questions that have to be asked:

- Who is affected by the thinking (action)? (Yellow Cap)
- What are the views (thinking) of those affected? (Blue Cap)

In doing an OPV we need to look at values and we need to be concerned with what others are actually thinking at this moment: we should not be concerned with what they should think.

The first step is to list the people affected and the second step is to imagine the views and thinking of each of those people affected.

Principles

■ You ought to be able to see the other point of view, whether or not you agree with it.

■ Every point of view may be right for the person having that viewpoint but it may not be right enough to be imposed on others.

■ Different people have different positions, backgrounds, knowledge, interests, values and wants and so their viewpoints can differ.

Project

Other ideas that can be substituted for any one or more of the above items or used as follow-up activities/homework.

■ There is a train strike and people find it difficult to get to work. How many different points of view are involved in this situation?

■ Do an OPV on someone who has just realised he is on the wrong aeroplane, going to the wrong place.

■ There is a minor traffic accident. The drivers start shouting at each other and eventually begin fighting. Do an OPV for each driver.

■ A boy gives some money to his older friend to buy a lottery ticket. The friend buys two tickets. One of the tickets is the winning ticket for a large amount of money. Which boy does the winning ticket belong to? Do an OPV on this situation.

■ A girl wants to get her own way. She goes on a hunger strike and refuses to eat anything. Do an OPV.

Practising using OPV – Lesson 12, Worksheet 44

Other People's Views

A father forbids his 13 year old daughter to smoke.

What is the father's point of view?

What is the daughter's point of view?

The father's point of view could be that:

_____

_____

_____

_____

_____

_____

_____

The daughter's point of view could be that:

_____

_____

_____

_____

_____

_____

_____

_____

After 5 minutes we will discuss this with the rest of the class.

Practising using OPV – Lesson 12, Worksheet 45

Other People's Views

A boy refuses to obey his teacher in class. The teacher reports the boy to the head teacher who excludes him. The boy's parents object.

- ● What are the boy's viewpoints?
- ● What are the teacher's viewpoints?
- ● What are the head teacher's viewpoints?
- ● What are the viewpoints of the class?

Underline the point of view that you have been asked to discuss.

The .... point of view could be that:

_____

_____

_____

_____

_____

_____

_____

_____

_____

_____

_____

_____

After 5 minutes we will discuss this with the rest of the class.

Practising using OPV – Lesson 12, Worksheet 46

Other People's Views

A girl likes to do her homework listening to loud music. She doesn't want to use earphones. Her parents and her brother like to work in peace and quiet. Do an OPV on this situation from:

- the girl's point of view
- the brother's point of view
- the parents' point of view.

Underline the point of view that you have been asked to discuss.

The .... point of view could be that:

_____

_____

_____

_____

_____

_____

_____

_____

_____

_____

_____

_____

_____

_____

_____

After 5 minutes we will discuss this with the rest of the class.

Appendix
Posters

The Six Thinking Caps

Plus Minus Interest (PMI)

Consider All Factors (CAF)

Rules

Consequences and Sequel (C&S)

Aims, Goals and Objectives (AGO)

Planning

First Important Priorities (FIP)

Alternatives, Possibilities, Choices (APC)

Decisions

Other People's Views (OPV)

These posters are all available in full colour to print out from the CD-ROM supplied with this book.

White Cap

Neutral, objective, getting information

Red Cap

R

Emotions, feelings, hunches

Black Cap

Cautious, careful
What are the weaknesses, dangers, problems?

Yellow Cap

Optimistic and positive

What are the advantages and benefits?

Will it work?

Green Cap

Action – making things happen, new and alternative ideas

Blue Cap

Taking control and organising

PMI

The Treatment of Ideas

Plus
- The good things about an idea

Minus
- The bad things about an idea

Interest
- Where these ideas might lead or what might happen

Consider All Factors

Factors affecting ourselves

●

Factors affecting others

●

Factors affecting our community

●

Factors affecting society

Rules

Why do we have them?

To prevent confusion
(e.g. road safety)

To assist enjoyment
(e.g. rules of a game)

To protect society
(e.g. laws)

The purpose of a rule is to make life easier and better for the majority of people.

C & S

Consequences and Sequel

The process of looking and thinking ahead: Focusing directly on the future and asking…

What happens after the decision has been made?

Thinking ahead and focusing directly on the future

It's different from CAF – this looks at the factors at the time of making a decision.

AGO

Aims, Goals and Objectives

We can do something

- out of habit

- because everyone else does it

- as an immediate reaction

Sometimes we do something *in order* to achieve:

- a goal

- an aim

- an objective

Planning

Planning is thinking ahead to see how you are going to do something, to achieve what you want to achieve.

It can be as simple as

- getting to some place

or in the longer term like

- getting the job you want as an adult

FIP

First Important Priorities

Some things are more important than others

In thinking about decisions we might take, when there are lots of ideas...

...we have to decide which are the important ones so we can do something about them!

APC

Alternatives, Possibilities, Choices

When making choices or decisions there are often more alternatives than we first think.

APC means we should look carefully at all the details and see if there are other explanations.

Decisions

Some decisions are easy and some are more difficult, but all decisions are important as they all have consequences.

In making decisions it is useful if you have considered the:

- factors involved (CAF)
- objectives (AGO)
- priorities (FIP)
- consequences (C&S)
- alternatives (APC)

Other People's Views

**Most thinking involves
other people.**

**What other people think is
as important to a situation
as the factors involved.**

**Other people may have a
different viewpoint from us.**